GREAT ARTISTS

MICHELANGELO

Roberto Carvalho de Magalhães

ENCHANTED LION BOOKS
New York

Michelangelo Buonarroti

IN THESE YEARS

1490 Michelangelo goes to live as a guest in the Palazzo Medici, staying until 1492. At this time, under Lorenzo de' Medici, "the Magnificent" (grandson of Cosimo the Elder), Florence is "the cradle of the Renaissance."

1492 Death of Lorenzo de' Medici.

Columbus sails to the New World.

1494 Michelangelo gives the prior of the convent of Santo Spirito a wooden crucifix (now displayed in the sacristy of the church), perhaps to thank him for making available a room and some corpses for his study of human anatomy.

The artist goes to Bologna, where he is received by Gianfrancesco Aldovrandi, and makes three sculptures for the church of San Domenico.

1495 Returns to Florence. He stays in the house of Lorenzo di Pierfrancesco de' Medici.

1496 In June, the artist goes to Rome for the first time.

Michelangelo has been accorded almost mythical status as an artist ever since the publication of Giorgio Vasari's *Lives of the Artists* in the sixteenth century. The powerful figures in his frescoes and sculptures reflect a boundless artistic energy that has made his art both unique and universal, creating a standard by which all artists measure themselves.

Michelangelo was born in Caprese, a village in Tuscany, on March 6, 1475. As an artist, he was inspired by the early Florentine masters Giotto and Masaccio. In 1488, he began an apprenticeship in Ghirlandaio's workshop, but left after a year to devote his energies to sculpture. Lorenzo de' Medici was Michelangelo's first real patron, taking him into his home in the Palazzo Medici-Riccardi and letting him work in the gardens of San Marco, where the talented young artist made copies of classical statues. At this point, the unstable political situation in Florence induced Michelangelo (aged only nineteen) to move to Bologna. Two years later he made his first trip to Rome, where he was to spend much of his life and where he produced most of his sculpture, painting and architecture. In 1546, he was put in charge of the building of St Peter's in Rome. Although physically infirm, Michelangelo never stopped working and his last sculptures, including the *Rondanini Pietà*, were made in old age. According to a contemporary source, the aged artist "walks doubled up and raises his head with difficulty, but continues stonecutting in his house." He died in Rome on February 18, 1564. This book is concerned only with his painting and sculpture.

Madonna della Scala

In what is believed to be his first work in marble, the Madonna holding the Child is seated at the foot of a flight of stairs (hence the title, "Madonna of the Stairs"), on which cherubs are playing. The young sculptor has taken his inspiration from the motif of the *Virgo lactans*, or Mary breastfeeding Jesus, a subject that was often shown on ancient sarcophagi, Greek reliefs, classical gems and funerary stelae. Unlike most representations of the Madonna and Child, this one has the Virgin looking straight ahead, while the baby Jesus seems to be asleep, with his right arm curled limply behind his back. Despite the stillness of the two figures, the scene is filled with tension. This derives from the vibrant contours of the sculpted lines, especially in the Madonna's clothes, but also from the circular movement generated by the position of the arms of Mary and Jesus. The relief uses a technique developed by Donatello known as *stiacciato* (literally, "squashed"), which achieves the maximum effect of spatial depth with the minimum of relief carving. From close up,

the figures and the architecture do indeed seem to be squashed, but from the right distance and with the effect of chiaroscuro, they assume volume and create the illusion of space.

Madonna della Scala
1489–92, marble,
21¹/₂ x 15¹/₂ in.
(55¹/₂ x 40 cm.)
Florence, Casa Buonarroti

The satyr is usually included in representations of the god Bacchus. In classical mythology he represents the instincts in man that are opposed to reason. This is why he is shown with goat's feet, tail, and horns – allusions to his bestial nature, which is governed by instinct.

MEDICI PATRONAGE AND THE CLASSICAL WORLD

The Medici family gave constant encouragement to the study of the arts of classical antiquity, without which it would have been impossible for Michelangelo to create such innovative sculptures as the *Battle of the Centaurs* (Casa Buonarroti) or *Bacchus*. In Florence, Michelangelo was able to study the statues in Lorenzo the Magnificent's collection and it was with a letter of recommendation from Pierfrancesco de' Medici that the artist journeyed to Rome and was received by Cardinal Riario. The *Bacchus* was made for the cardinal, although he refused the finished piece and it was later acquired by the banker, Jacopo Galli.

Bacchus

Michelangelo had studied human anatomy at the convent of Santo Spirito in Florence, thanks to the co-operation of the prior who allowed him to study corpses. In addition to its evident borrowings from antique statuary (both in the subject and pose), this *Bacchus* – made in Rome when Michelangelo was only twenty-two – shows careful attention to anatomical detail, especially in the slight movement of the young god, who seems to be swaying

under the influence of wine. This sculpture has little of the tension and drama usually found in Michelangelo's work. Rather, here the artist has placed the emphasis on the ambiguous sensuality of the god, with his smooth skin and effeminate features. Bacchus's traditional attributes are all shown: the grapes, the cup of wine and the small satyr. The little figure, twisting round to nibble the grapes held in the god's left hand, adds life to the sculpture.

Bacchus
1496–97, marble,
h. 72¼ in. (84 cm.)
79¾ in. (203 cm.) with base
Florence, Rargello

IN THESE YEARS

1496 In Rome, Michelangelo is the guest of Cardinal Riario, collector of antiquities and cousin of the future Pope Julius II, for about a year.

1497 Cardinal Jean Bilhères de Lagraulas commissions the *Pietà* from the artist, a piece which now resides in St Peter's, in the Vatican City, Rome.

The first restoration of the Pietà, *involving the right hand of Christ, was carried out in 1736, before the statue was moved to its present location. On May 21, 1972 (Whit Sunday), a madman struck the statue fifteen times with a hammer, and another lengthy restoration was required.*

Pietà

The most immediate precedents for Michelangelo's *Pietà*, which shows the Virgin holding the large, lifeless body of her son on her lap, are perhaps to be sought in the paintings of the late-fifteenth century artists Cosmè Tura and Ercole de' Roberti of Ferrara. In this work, we are struck by the extreme youth of the Virgin cradling an adult Christ in her lap. This was explained, in the sixteenth century, as symbolizing the immaculateness of Mary, who bore none of the physical signs of sin. The sculpture has stood in the first chapel in the right aisle of St Peter's in Rome since 1749. It is the only one of the artist's works to bear his signature: on the ribbon crossing the Virgin's breast we read: MICHEL. ANGELUS.

BONAROTUS. FLORENT. FACIEBAT. The expression of absorbed resignation on Mary's face combines here with the dynamism of opposing forces that is so typical of Michelangelo's work. Christ's body seems as though it is about to fall, even though his resting head faces upward toward heaven. The Virgin and the folds of her clothing convey an upward movement, determined by her effort to support her son, while her gaze is cast downward. The power of Michelangelo's work derives from these opposing tendencies.

Pietà
1498–99, marble,
h. 68¼ in. (174 cm.)
76½ in. (195 cm.) with
base)
Rome, St Peter's

IN THESE YEARS

1501 Michelangelo returns to Florence. He signs a contract to produce fifteen statues for Siena Cathedral. The Wool Weavers' Guild commissions *David*.

1503 Leonardo da Vinci paints the *Mona Lisa*. The Wool Weavers' Guild commissions statues of the Twelve Apostles for Florence

David

For this huge, powerful statue, Michelangelo used an enormous block of Carrara marble that the Opera del Duomo had made available to him, and on which other sculptors had labored in vain during the fifteenth century. The Old Testament biblical hero, who freed the Hebrew people by slaying the giant Goliath with a stone from his sling, is not shown in action. In fact, he lacks the traditional attributes of a sword and helmet with which he is usually associated, and rests his prodigious sling over his left shoulder with an apparent air of nonchalance. In Michelangelo's sculpture, David himself becomes the giant — his massive hands and forceful gaze symbolizing both his moral strength and his intelligence. In this sculpture, Michelangelo has employed all his knowledge

Cathedral, but only work on the statue of *St. Matthew* is started.

1504 *David* is set up in the Piazza della

Signoria. In 1873, the original is moved to the Accademia, and in 1910 a marble copy is set up in the piazza.

of human anatomy and classical art. The pose itself recalls that of athletes in classical Greek sculpture, although in this statue the turn of the head to the left, in contrast to the frontal stance of the body, reveals an almost frightening energy. The statue was originally placed to one side of the entrance of the Palazzo Vecchio, in the Piazza della Signoria, the main square in Florence. It was moved in 1873 to the Galleria dell'Accademia. In 1910, a copy was placed in front of the Palazzo Vecchio. Another copy stands vigil over the city, from the Piazzale Michelangelo.

David
1501–04,
marble,
h. 161¼ in. (410 cm.)
170½ in. (434 cm.) with base
Florence, Galleria dell'Accademia

Tondo Pitti (Virgin and Child with the Young St John)

This marble tondo, commissioned by the Florentine Bartolomeo Pitti (after whom it is named), is another masterpiece based on contrasting rhythms and psychology. It shows Mary seated with her son standing by her side. The Child, who rests his right elbow on an open book, has a joyful expression. His pose follows the curved edge of the relief. The figure of Mary, on the other hand, emerges from the vertical and horizontal lines of her arm and leg. Her body is turned toward her son, but her head, with its somewhat troubled expression, is turned away. The contrasting attitudes of the two figures are made to stand out from the rest of the composition – executed for the most part in the *stiacciato* technique – through the deeper carving of their heads. This articulated interplay of contrasts, underscored by the diagonal insertion of a straight-cut shape – the cube on which the Madonna is sitting – fills the tondo with both pulsing energy and inexorable movement.

**Tondo Pitti
(Virgin and Child
with the Young St John)**
1503–05,
marble, 33$\frac{1}{2}$ x 32$\frac{1}{4}$ in.
(85$\frac{1}{2}$ x 82 cm.),
Florence, Bargello

IN THESE YEARS

1505 Michelangelo is commissioned to design the tomb for Pope Julius II, and

goes to Carrara to choose the marble.

1506 In January, the artist is in Rome, but he is not received by

the pope, who refuses to confirm the commission for the tomb. Thus begins the stormy relationship between Michelangelo

and Pope Julius. Leonardo da Vinci and Michelangelo are summoned to Florence to paint frescoes in the Palazzo Vecchio

representing two Florentine victories. Leonardo is to paint the Battle of Anghiari, Michelangelo the Battle of Cascina.

Tondo Doni (The Holy Family with the Infant St John the Baptist)

The *Tondo Doni*, the only surviving panel painting that can be attributed with certainty to Michelangelo, was probably painted on the occasion of the wedding of the rich Florentine merchant Agnolo Doni and Maddalena Strozzi that took place in 1503 or 1504. The frame, with its five projecting heads (delineating an ideal pentagon), may have been designed by Michelangelo himself. The composition is divided into two planes. In the foreground, Mary is sitting on the grass and turning backward to take her son, who is being passed to her by Joseph. Her movement, through the opposition between the lines of her arms and her legs, creates a spiral. The figure of Joseph, whose legs are improbably wide apart, acts as a back-rest for her. The group is compact and dynamic, yet harmonious. In the background, inside a hexagonal enclosure, a number of male nudes can be seen chatting in an animated fashion. This juxtaposition has been interpreted as an allegory of humanity before (the background figures) and after the arrival of Christianity, embodied by the Holy Family in the foreground. The infant St John, to the right, seems to be acting as an intermediary between these two worlds.

Tondo Doni (Holy Family with the Infant St John the Baptist)
1506–07, tempera on panel, diameter
47¼ in. (120 cm.), *Florence, Uffizi Gallery*

The magnificently carved frame adds to the composition of the painting, most notably in the triangle formed by the head at the top and the two at the bottom.

The Creation of Adam

The most famous scene on the ceiling of the Sistine Chapel occupies a central position on the immense painted vault (though the *Creation of Eve* is in the exact center). Adam is brought to life by God the Father who glides forth, surrounded by angels – some of them supporting him, others gathering with curiosity about his shoulders. The Earth is represented by an unidentified green surface on which the progenitor of the human race reclines. The Swiss Romantic painter Henry Fuseli described the touching of the two fingers as an electric charge that brings life into being. Indeed, the

scene is charged with energy and imperious movement – in the Creator's gesture, in his long hair and flowing beard, and the big, red drapery that balloons behind him in a rush of wind. The vivacity of the divine figure and his entourage contrasts with the languid pose of the indolent Adam, who has just received the gift of life. Once again, as in all of his great frescoes and sculptures, Michelangelo twists his figures into poses that convey the tension and power of their bodies. Here, both God and Adam are twisting their torsos in the opposite direction from their legs. God's left arm encircles a woman's shoulders; this has been interpreted as heralding the creation of Eve.

The Creation of Adam
1510, fresco
110¹/₄ x 224¹/₄ in.
(280 x 570 cm.)
Rome, Vatican,
Sistine Chapel

The Fall of Man

Two episodes from the story of Adam and Eve are represented in this composition. On the left, Adam and Eve are shown among the luxuriant vegetation of the Garden of Eden. Eve, seated on the ground, twists her body in a fashion characteristic of Michelangelo in order to accept the forbidden fruit from the hand of the "serpent" (the Devil). On the right, the guilty pair are driven out of Paradise into a desolate

wilderness by a sword-wielding angel. Adam and Eve, who on the left appear young, now look much older, their faces aged by guilt. Old age is here taken as a symbol of sin, just as the surprising youthfulness of the Virgin in the Vatican *Pietà* is an expression of her purity. The tree in the center both separates and links the two scenes, which are also joined by the interplay of outstretched arms. There is a linear flow from left to right, which establishes a fluid continuity that underscores the narrative.

The Fall of Man
1509, fresco
$110^1/_4$ x $224^1/_4$ in.
(280 x 570 cm.)
Rome, Vatican, Sistine Chapel

IN THESE YEARS

1506 Michelangelo begins his fresco in the Palazzo Vecchio in November, but does not complete it. Leonardo withdraws from the project, after his experiments fail. His painting is irreparably damaged.

Michelangelo meets Julius II in Bologna. The pope orders a portrait of himself in bronze, to be set up on the façade of San Petronio.

1508 The statue of Julius II is installed in a niche above the doorway of the church in Bologna.

Michelangelo is in Rome from April onward, and is ordered to fresco the Sistine Chapel.

1509 The artist confides to his brother Bonarroto: "Here I am with many worries and with very great fatigue of body, and I do not have friends of any kind nor do I want any, and I do not have enough time to eat."

1511 The Bentivoglio family, who are hostile to Julius II, return to power in Bologna. His statue is destroyed.

The Flood

This was the first scene Michelangelo painted in the Sistine Chapel. He used assistants, including Bugiardini, who painted the figures at the sides, and Granacci, who executed the ones in the left foreground. But Michelangelo was not pleased with his pupils' work and continued the fresco on his own. The scene shows the Flood with the waters rising. Noah's Ark is visible in the background. Desperate groups of men, women and children, many laden with possessions, seek refuge on any remaining dry land. The Ark is

surrounded by those who have been shut out. Some try to help each other, while others fight furiously for a place in the boat in the center, or in the Ark itself. The entire, agitated scene shows episodes of egoism and compassion, and of love and loathing. In 1797, an explosion at the nearby Castel Sant' Angelo damaged this part of the ceiling, and the upper right portion of the scene was lost.

According to contemporary accounts, it showed God's anger in the form of a thunderbolt. While producing *The Flood*, Michelangelo may have been thinking of the similarly dramatic version of the subject painted by Paolo Uccello in the cloister of Santa Maria Novella, in Florence.

The Flood
1508–09, fresco,
106¹/₄ x 224¹/₄ in.
(270 x 570 cm.)
Rome, Vatican, Sistine Chapel

The Sistine Chapel

With her statuesque pose, the Delphic Sibyl recalls the figure of the Madonna in the Tondo Pitti, *which Michelangelo had painted in 1506–07.*

The gigantic fresco that covers the ceiling of the Sistine Chapel – a Cyclopean work that Michelangelo painted almost entirely by his own hand – was commissioned by Pope Julius II, for whom the artist had already made a bronze statue (later destroyed) for the façade of the church of San Petronio in Bologna. The enormous room of over 1,600 square feet (500 square meters) had been built for Pope Sixtus IV (and is therefore known as the Sixtine, or Sistine, Chapel). Among the first painters who worked on the decoration were Botticelli, Perugino, Signorelli and Ghirlandaio (Michelangelo's first master). They had painted stories from the life of Moses and the life of Christ around the walls of the huge room. Michelangelo's monumental fresco was to go above, and was to replace the starry heavens painted on the ceiling by Piermatteo d'Amelia. There is no agreement on the question of who devised the complex iconographic scheme. Some scholars believe that it was Michelangelo himself, who based the design on the Old Testament sequence of episodes and Prophets, then added in the Sibyls in reference to the Greek

Ceiling Design
1. The Creation of Light
2. The Creation of Stars and Planets
3. Separation of the Earth from the Waters
4. The Creation of Adam
5. The Creation of Eve
6. The Fall of Man
7. The Sacrifice of Noah
8. The Flood
9. The Drunkenness of Noah
10. Ignudo (nude male figure)

tradition. In order to give form to the nine scenes from Genesis that fill the central band of the ceiling, the artist devised a trompe l'oeil architectural structure that not only divided the surface into compartments for the episodes, but also served to amplify it. In this way, he was able to insert 300 or so figures: from the smallest, represented by the cherubs who act as caryatids to support the architectural structure and the scenes of Creation, to the largest, such as the Prophets and Sibyls, which are almost eighteen feet (three meters) tall. The biblical episodes are painted in brilliant, joyful colors. The figures' drapery, especially that of the Prophets and Sibyls, features variable color, in which green mutates into red or yellow, and blue into orange. So in addition to the architectural and sculptural elements, there is a masterly use of color in this work, the greatest of all pictorial cycles.

The figures of the Sibyls and Prophets, such as this one of Daniel, have immense sculptural presence and seem to burst out of the architecture that encloses them.

pages 22–23: **The Sistine Chapel (overall view of the ceiling)** *1508–12*
Rome, Vatican

● *The Prophets* ■ *Ancestors of Christ*
● *The Sibyls* *Scenes from Genesis*

Michelangelo called the pairs of nude youths on the Sistine ceiling "Ignudi," and his term is still used by art historians for this particular subject.

Separation of the Earth from the Waters
1511, fresco,
155¹/₄ x 78¹/₂ in.
(395 x 200 cm.)
Rome, Vatican, Sistine Chapel

Separation of the Earth from the Waters

This scene is generally believed to show the separation of the waters as described in Genesis, but some critics think that it shows the creation of aquatic animals, or animals in general. In any case, it is one of five episodes which show the appearance of God. The other images are all devoted to the "human miseries," beginning with the original sin. Some scholars, noting that the division of the ceiling into these two fundamental parts corresponds to the original division, at ground level, between the sanctuary and the area intended for the lay congregation, have rightly discerned a theological basis for the arrangement. The scenes with God (including the *Separation of the Earth*), are near the altar, where mass is celebrated. The scenes of human misery, more suited to sinners, are above the congregation. In this fresco, the figure of God is dynamically foreshortened, making his gesture even more majestic. Like all the scenes in the central part of the ceiling, this one is surrounded by four "Ignudi" in a variety of poses. These are both virtuoso studies and decorative features that help to animate the entire cycle.

Michelangelo's first architectural work, the *New Sacristy* in the church of San Lorenzo in Florence, constitutes an entire architectural, sculptural, spatial and pictorial universe. It is a poetic meditation on the understanding of man and on the mystery of life and death. Designed at the request of Cardinal Giuliano de' Medici and Pope Leo X, it was produced between 1521 and 1534. It was finished, after Michelangelo's final departure from Florence, by Vasari and Ammanati. It is called the *New Sacristy* to distinguish it from Brunelleschi's *Old Sacristy*, of which it forms the pendant. Both sacristies have the same plan – a square space surmounted by a cupola. The very tall walls enlivened with perspective effects, including the paired pilasters, form the backdrop to the funerary monuments of Lorenzo (1492–1519) and Giuliano de' Medici (1479–1516).

Dawn and Dusk

In his *Life of Michelangelo Buonarroti* of 1553, Ascanio Condivi refers to the sculptural cycle in the *New Sacristy* at San Lorenzo as a representation of "time that consumes all things." Four allegorical statues are placed on the tombs of two short-lived members of the Medici dynasty. They symbolize the hours of the day, and therefore the time that passes. *Dawn* and *Dusk* are on the tomb of Lorenzo, Duke of Urbino. Here, too, Michelangelo makes use of the formal and thematic contrasts already noted in his previous works. The young female figure of *Dawn* seems to be rousing herself from sleep and wears a melancholy expression. The treatment of her extremely elongated body, which the sculptor has twisted slightly, goes beyond mere anatomical observation to express a rhythm, a state of the soul. She is complemented by *Dusk*, personified as a powerful old man, whose pose is similar but reversed, and which has the same torsion. The very beautiful head of the old man was left unfinished by Michelangelo.

The statue of Lorenzo, Duke of Urbino, son of Piero de' Medici and grandson of Lorenzo the Magnificent, is in the niche above the sarcophagus.

Dawn and Dusk
1524–31, marble,
l. 81 in. (206 cm.) each
Florence, San Lorenzo, New Sacristy

Julius II. The contract for the making of his tomb is confirmed in his will.
1517 At the request of Pope Leo X,

Michelangelo makes designs and a model for the façade of the unfinished church of San Lorenzo in Florence. To

Michelangelo's immense annoyance, and for reasons that are unclear, the pope cancels the whole project in 1520.

Night and Day

The tomb of Giuliano, Duke of Nemours, third child of Lorenzo the Magnificent, is surmounted by sculptures of *Night* and *Day*, which are both antithetical and complementary to one another. The figure for *Night*, a sleeping woman, shows considerable torsion (like the Madonna in the *Tondo Doni* and many of the Sistine Chapel figures). In a way that increases the sculpture's tension, her bent right arm is contrasted with the shape of her raised left leg. The mirror-

The statue of Giuliano, Duke of Nemours, is inside the niche above the sarcophagus. The anatomical deformation to which Michelangelo subjected his figures is apparent in Giuliano's neck, which is elongated far beyond reality.

image of her pose is used for the male figure of *Day*, whose massive, unfinished head gazes directly at the observer. This pair is on the other side of the room from the tomb featuring *Dawn* and *Dusk*, and is in perfect symmetry with it. Thus, through similarities and contrasts, and with increasing and decreasing movement, Michelangelo constructs his allegory of human existence.

Night and Day
1524–31, marble,
l. 76½ in.
(195 cm.) each
Florence, San Lorenzo,
New Sacristy

IN THESE YEARS

1524 Michelangelo is commissioned to build the Laurentian Library in Florence.
1528 Death of Buonarroto, Michelangelo's favorite brother.

Madonna and Child (Medici Madonna)

This is yet another Madonna and Child in which, as we have seen in the *Madonna della Scala* and the *Tondo Pitti*, the Mother is shown looking away from the son she holds, her gaze troubled, as though agonized by a premonition of Jesus's destiny. The sculpture stands on the right-hand wall of the *New Sacristy* in San Lorenzo and, together with the statues of St Cosmas and St Damian, it completes Michelangelo's sculptural cycle.

This group, too, is rendered lively and full of tension by the contrasting movements of the two figures. The Child twists backward in search of the breast and leans slightly to the left. The Virgin offers her left breast with a slight contrary movement, while her head, its gaze directed far into the distance, is tilted slightly to our right. Infant vivacity and maternal presentiment seem to condense the message of life and death conveyed by the other sculptures in the *New Sacristy*.

Madonna and Child (Medici Madonna)
1521–34, marble,
h. 88³/₄ in. (226 cm.)
Florence, San Lorenzo,
New Sacristy

The Last Judgement

Michelangelo painted the wall behind the papal high altar of the Sistine Chapel with the *Last Judgement*, a vast fresco comprising some 400 figures – many identifiable, some not. The composition is based on large groups, which are then subdivided into smaller ones. The upper portion of the fresco shows the Court of Heaven. In the center, Christ the Judge, flanked by the Virgin, are the hub of the whole composition. At their sides are serried ranks of patriarchs and apostles. To the left and right of them, at the same height but rendered more distant by the perspective, we find the martyrs, confessors, virgins and saints. Above, in the two lunettes, powerful angels bear the symbols of the Passion. At Christ's feet, seated on clouds, are the two martyr saints, Lawrence and Bartholomew. In the register immediately below, on the left, we see those who are ascending to heaven after the Judgement, and on the right, the dramatic and terrible scene of those who are being taken down to hell. Between these two groups are the angels, who awaken the dead from their tombs. In the lower register, on the left, the resurrection of the dead can be seen, and on the right, Charon ferrying the souls of the damned.

Who's who
1. Christ; 2. The Virgin; 3. St Paul; 4. St Peter; 5. Job; 6. Abel
7. The Archangel Gabriel; 8. St Bartholomew; 9. Charon; 10. Minos.

More than twenty-one years after completing the great fresco on the ceiling, Michelangelo painted the end wall with the Last Judgement, *for Pope Paul III.*

The Last Judgement
1536–41, fresco, 539¹/₄ x 480¹/₄ in. (1370 x 1220 cm.)
Rome, Vatican, Sistine Chapel

1529 Florence is threatened with invasion by the papal armies. Michelangelo is put in charge of the city's defense strategy.

1532 In Rome, the artist forms a romantic friendship with Tommaso de' Cavalieri, to whom he dedicates drawings and sonnets.

1538 Michelangelo is charged with the task of setting up the bronze equestrian statue of Marcus Aurelius on the Capitoline Hill in Rome.

1542 The artist begins the frescoes *Conversion of St Paul* and the *Martyrdom of St Peter* in the Pauline Chapel in the Vatican.

1545 The Council of Trent opens, as a reaction against the Protestant Reformation. It will last until 1563.

1546 Michelangelo is put in charge of the building of St Peter's Basilica and of the completion of both the Palazzo Farnese and the fortification of the Borgo.

St. Bartholemew, The Last Judgement
(detail) 1536-1541,
fresco,
1370 x 1220 cm,
*Rome, Vatican,
Sistine Chapel*

St Bartholomew, who was flayed alive, holds limp human skin in his left hand. It has been suggested that the crumpled face on the empty skin is that of Michelangelo himself.

The half of his face not covered by his hand expresses all the terror felt by this powerfully built man at the realization of his fate.

One of the Condemned, The Last Judgement
(detail)
1536-1541,
fresco,
1370 x 1220 cm
*Rome, Vatican,
Sistine Chapel*

Animals are extremely rare in Michelangelo's work. There are none even in his fresco of the Flood. The inclusion of Saul's horse in this fresco is highly unusual.

Conversion of St Paul

c. 1542–45, fresco, 246 x 260¹/₄ in. (625 x 661 cm.)

Rome, Vatican, Pauline Chapel

Conversion of St. Paul

Michelangelo completed his last fresco cycle at the age of seventy-five. It consists of two large scenes: the *Conversion of St Paul* and the *Crucifixion of St Peter.* These frescoes were commissioned by Pope Paul III for his private chapel in the Vatican, now known as the Pauline Chapel. The choice of the two saints is significant: Peter was the founder of the church and became the first pope, whereas Saul, a renown persecutor of Christians, fell from his horse on the road to Damascus when a divine light shone in his eyes. Converted to Christianity, he took the name of Paul. This fresco not only tells the Apostle's story, but is also an act of homage to the pope. This is a very busy, agitated scene. A beam of light unites the figure of Christ above with that of Saul stretched out on the ground below. Each is surrounded by animated groups of moving figures. Those of the angels converge on the Savior, while those of the mortals seem to flee to the left and the right in terror. Once again Michelangelo has used opposing forces to express the dramatic quality of the event he is depicting.

IN THESE YEARS	Florence, in which he hails Michelangelo as the greatest artist of all time.	last works, including the *Rondanini Pietà*.	The Congregation of the Council of Trent decides that the nude figures in the Sistine Chapel must be covered up.	**1564** Michelangelo dies in Rome, nearly eighty-nine years of age.
1550 Giorgio Vasari publishes the first edition of his famous *Lives of the Artists* in	**1550–64** The aged sculptor produces his	**1558** He makes the wooden model for the dome of St Peter's.		

Pietà (Rondanini Pietà)

According to Michelangelo's first biographers, Vasari and Condivi, the sculptor began this work to adorn his own tomb, which at one time he wanted to be in the church of Santa Maria Maggiore in Rome. Its making was fraught with difficulties, and on one occasion the left leg of the Christ figure was broken. Michelangelo left the sculpture unfinished, and it was continued by Tiberio Calcagni, who worked especially on the figure of the Magdalene, on Christ's right. The extreme torsion to which Michelangelo liked to submit the human body reappears in the figure of Christ: it is more pronounced than ever here, dictated as it is by the inertia of his lifeless body, which slips as Nicodemus, the Virgin and Mary Magdalene try to lift it. Michelangelo is perhaps thinking of certain late fifteenth-century Florentine paintings, such as the moving and dramatic *Depositions* by Botticelli, in which the figures are linked together by an intricate interweaving of arms and hands.

Art historians have discerned Michelangelo's self-portrait in the features of Nicodemus, as well as in those of Saul in the Pauline Chapel. This idea receives support from a passage in a letter written by Vasari in the year of the artist's death: "there is an old man, in which he portrayed himself."

Pietà (Rondanini)
1550–55, marble,
h. 88³/₄ in. (226 cm.)
*Florence, Opera del
Duomo Museum*

Index of Michelangelo's works:

*The numbers in bold refer to pages where the work is reproduced.

First American edition published in 2003 by
Enchanted Lion Books
115 West 18th Street, New York, NY 10011
Copyright © 2002 McRae Books Srl
English language text copyright © 2003 McRae Books Srl
All rights reserved
Printed and bound in the Slovak Republic

Library of Congress Cataloging-in-Publication Data
Magalhaes, Roberto Carvalho de.
 Michelangelo / Roberto Carvalho de Magalhaes.
 p.cm — (Great artists)
 Includes index.
 Summary: Discusses the style and technique of the Italian Renaissance painter and sculptor, Michelangelo Buonarroti.
 ISBN 1-59270-008-X
 1. Michelangelo Buonarroti, 1475-1564—Criticism and interpretation—Juvenile literature. [1. Michelangelo Buonarroti, 1475-1564. 2. Artist.] I. Michelangelo Buonarroti, 1475-1564. II. Title. III Great artists (Enchanted Lion Books)
 N6923.B9M28 2003
 709'.2—dc21   2003048911

The series "Great Artists" was created and produced by
McRae Books Srl, Borgo Santa Croce, 8, Florence, Italy
Info@mcraebooks.com
Series Editor: Roberto Carvalho de Magalhães
Text: Roberto Carvalho de Magalhães
Design: Marco Nardi · Layouts: Laura Ottina
The Publisher thanks the following archives, which authorized the reproduction of the artwork depicted in this volume: Scala Group, Florence (3, 4-5, 6-7, 10-11, 12, 15, 16-17, 19, 20-21, 23, 24, 25, 26, 27, 28, 29, 30, 31, 33, 35, 37, 39),
Bridgeman Art Library, London (9, 34).

Cover: **The Sistine Chapel,** (overall view of the ceiling), 1508-1512, (detail)
Page 1: **The Last Judgement,** 1536-1541, (detail)